Anecdotal Evidence: Millennial Whining & Wisdom

Kristin Frederick

BookLeaf Publishing

Presentation by *BookLeaf Publishing*

Web: www.bookleafpub.com

E-mail: info@bookleafpub.com

ISBN: 9789358368093

First edition 2023

A modern legacy, mainly aimed toward my kids and siblings, but also anyone with a sense of humor and curiosity. Keep living life the way you want to.

ACKNOWLEDGEMENT

Words cannot express my gratitude to my husband Kyle, who has always hyped me up to have fun, even if that means poetry. Also to my Spotify account, which helps keep me sane with the sounds of Brendon Urie of Panic! at the Disco, Lady Gaga, Patrick Stump of Fall Out Boy, and Lizzo, who are all poets in their own right.

PREFACE

Writing has always been a form of expression in my life, whether through journals, blogs, poetry, or social media. I loved it so much, I was scared to make it my job, because people hate their jobs. I went the opposite direction and got into finance just to be safe.

Today, I do not hate my finance job, and still enjoy writing, so win-win for me. My life has been unhinged enough that I figured I could tie my experiences in with humanity through the ebb and flow of poetry. I hope this proves to be entertaining and touching.

NPC Energy

(NPC: noun; In a video game, a "non-player character", whose presence isn't necessary to move the plot along, has the same repeating lines of script, and cannot interact with other characters.)

Up again, lift my body off the shelf
Stiff arms, not clearly seeing
Another day as a "human being".

Glance at my watch
Driving, cleaning, calling
Deja vu is my wonderful darling

Plugged into disconnection
Stale colors, stale sleep, stale air
Did the same thing yesterday, I swear

Everything is new but
No passion, no drive
Am I even really alive?

Up again, lift my body off the shelf
I think "Not much different than an NPC"

But... computer software did not design me.

I gain some introspection
Slide away from this embrace
See the separation, and abruptly change my pace

INTENTIONALLY I reach out, pursue, renew
Light my candles, go for walks,
Buy the ridiculous printed socks

Air is moving
Colors are brighter
My spirit and muscles are lifetimes lighter.

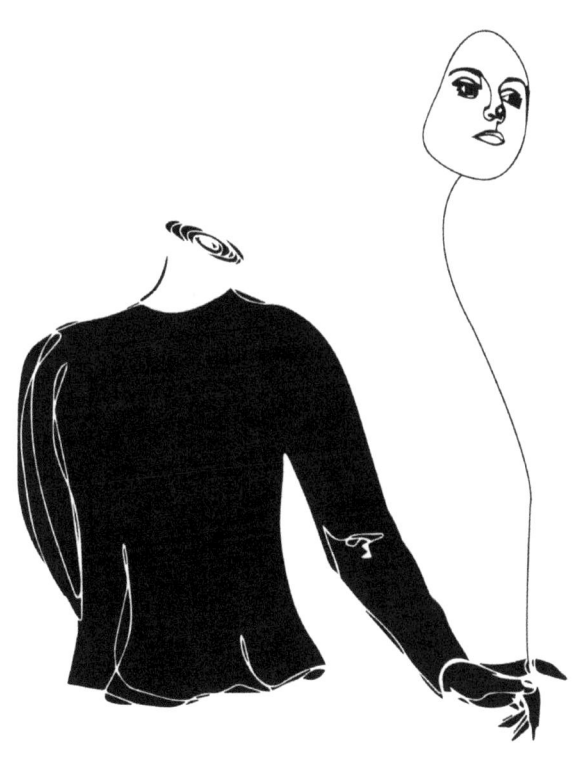

That Uneasy Feeling

9 years old, 3:45 PM
Streaming tears say "Bleak & dim"
This week was especially tough,
Fun plans falling through, & expectations are rough.
Heart beating fast, shaking, can't catch your breath
Skin crawling, fingers gripping, humanity fades, now you're deaf.
"What's happening to me?!"
"This is what's called anxiety"

That uneasy feeling? Like there's no control?
Stop now, let your thoughts unroll.

One breath, close your eyes, then uncurl your muscle
Give up what's left of your hustle.
No homework, chores, practices
Now make friends with your mattresses.
Blare your favorite song
Self-rescue now, sing along.
Take a hot bath, add epsom salt
Low lights, your bathroom is a sacred vault.
10 minutes later emerge - slowly
Soft clothes make recovery more cozy.

When you feel that uneasy feeling
Being kind to yourself is the first step in healing.

Do NOT Underestimate Music

(Cultural, social, emotional)
Humans can keep a beat, determine pitch,
differentiate sounds, and follow
melody simultaneously
Once the entire package is explored, wow, what
a gift to humanity!
A private world – unwanted versions of self are
shed,
No secrets survive, the lies have fled.

And the yearned versions of self? Woven to lore.
Stories, experiences, learned at our core.
Music brings everything back to life
As a skilled surgeon cutting cancer with a knife.

(Painful, hopeful, euphoric)

Music is ancestral experience as a sum
The closest to teleportation man has come.
We are taken to new heights, places, and designs
Human existence is not bound by time!
Music contains the secrets of life's pleasures
But can only be told in measures.

Through the physical and non-visible universe

Easily accessible in a purse
Infinite stories told through 5 lines, a clef, and shapes
Amazing & magical, one MUST partake!

When life has you confused about your role
Music's answers hit straight to the soul.

Truest Friends

Unsure if these friends are True or not?
The answer is not complicated and must be
sought.
True friends are comfortable anywhere.
From a shiny new club to a sleepover; they ALL
have flair.

Despite lots of money AND no money,
True friendship requires connection, time, and
delicate study.
True friends reciprocate unfiltered, supportive
comments.
They free you from life's consequential torment.

True friendship is a 2-way street
No relationship is perfect, but it shouldn't
deplete.
Time, gifts, favors, compliments
Must be exchanged with purest intent.

True friends respect your decisions but rescue
you when needed
It goldenly starts with "Treat others how you
want to be treated."

Fake friends are worse than honest enemies
So, communicate freely, openly, and clearly.

True friends are better not because of how
fantastic you are,
But because you've shown them how fantastic
they are.
True friends talk shit in person, and compliment
elsewhere.
Heed my warning: these True friends are RARE.

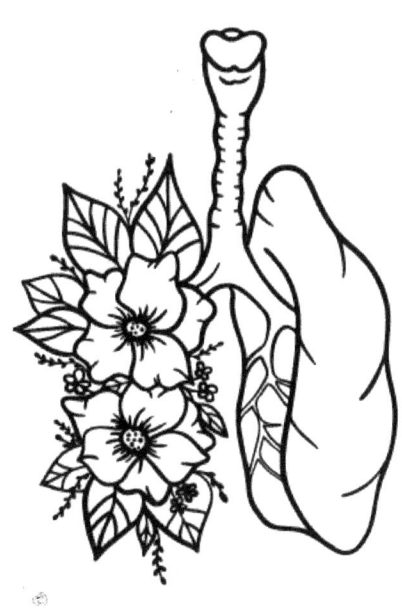

Your Prospective

From 13 to 99
Dating takes courage and spine
From being observant to staying clean
Introspection must be routine

Why are you wanting to date?
Make sure your prospective can also relate.

Don't be too serious,
Don't accept the slightest insult
Make no room for:
Disrespect, lies, opposition
Taking advantage, stealing, negativity

If any of these show up
Don't overthink, don't make excuses
For any reason you see fit, say to your
prospective:
"Thank you for your part in my life. This isn't
working out anymore."
Elaboration is up to you.
Release the relationship
And welcome new opportunities to cultivate
happiness

After all,
You must plant the strongest seeds now
For your best prospective

Commitment

Whether to a person, place or thing
Commitments are a weighty King

In this commitment certain peace MUST be
found:
Loyalty, ease, health, connection, common
ground
Consistency and personalities must not flip
Fun, prioritized time, and successful conflict

How?

When provocation comes and schemes
You and your commitment are a team.
It is the undesirable vs. the team,
NOT
You and the problem vs. your teammate

Don't talk bad about them to those close to you.
What an idiot you will be, starting your own
coup.

Admit when mistakes are made
Open up, even when afraid

Identify how not to repeat in the future

Seek advice as the first suture.

For some, privacy soothes,
For others, humor

Commitments are heavy,
When you sign up, make sure you can carry.

EXES

Past partners bring mixed emotions
smug
stupid
animosity
judgment
Nostalgia
Naivety
desperation
confusion
hurt
"What if?"
sadness
young
20/20 hindsight
experimentation
curiosity
growth
comfort
Letting go of barbed wire

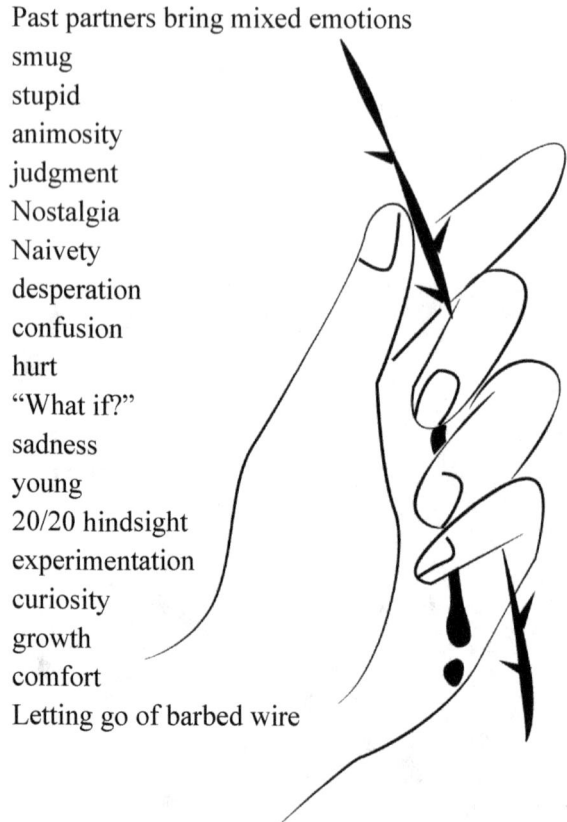

Wedding

Few things are a better display of the beauty in
life
Than a proper wedding
No matter how big or small,
Cheap or expensive,
Colorful or monotone,

A genuine vow and covenant
ALWAYS shines as the centerpiece.

A couple surrounded by unfeigned love &
support
This single day is one of the most supreme of
your life
So map it how you please
In a way that marks the start of the rest of your
days
Whether the worst or best -
It is what you make of the residue.

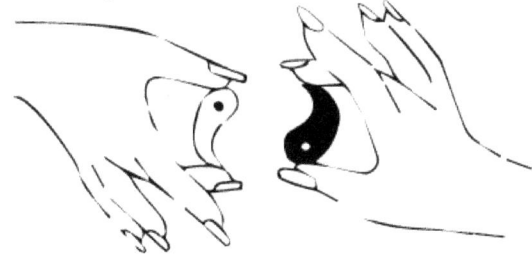

Anniversary

A vat of elbow grease goes into marriage.
Marriage is: function toward each other.
Marriage is: staying happy on purpose -
Not by being ignorant or passive
But by prioritizing the same values.

So it is absolutely necessary to stop and
celebrate
Another year of progress staying together.
Remember -
All the small things make up your daily life
And the spaces between make up your real life.

Make your anniversary lovely, alluring, splendid
For it is a reminder
of all the challenges you have and haven't yet
overcome.

Attitudes

The most inviting people aren't the richest,
Or the ones with stories to tell.
It's the people who have the best attitude
Who seldom have malice to quell.

The ones whose conversations
Are positive & uplifting,
Only rarely angry,
And emotions aren't violently shifting.

Who find the silver lining
Despite unfortunate circumstances
The best attitude
Despite being given zero chances

Not constantly complaining
About life, work, management
Happy to help people understand and improve
Without an expectation of debt

If you're ever stuck in a particular blunder
How much better could it be
With a small attitude reframe,
An adjustment of the key?
Whether you're looking for positive or negative
You will find what you are looking for.

Siblings

Being the oldest
There is a deep love and care for each sibling
Seeing you grow into your personalities
And fostering relationships with each other
That itself is an ever-bearing fruit tree.

The same house, people, and days
But slightly different memories...
These are a living breathing scrapbook
We all fashion unintentionally.

There is a flicker inside you
Seen for years
Along with your fears
But recall
You are powerful, strong
Your pain cannot take you

Because it is OF you!
Pain is actually your friend;
Protecting and communicating
That things are needing amends.

So when in pain
Turn to your siblings
When you need an extra set of ears.
Keep fashioning the scrapbook -
Automatic friends for years.

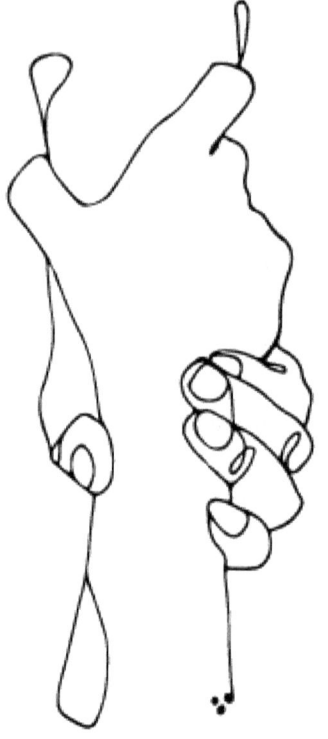

Give Kids the World

Kissimmee Florida
A quaint charming village,
Amusement park with some spunk
Ran by volunteers and charity
For kids with terminal illnesses

Make-a-Wish granted my brother's
And our family stayed here
No rules, just fun and memories

Mascots, ice cream, rides
Shows, music, and slides
Smiles on adults and children alike

Nighttime party had families gathered
Me, tired from the day's heat and itinerary
I sat down alone at a bench.

A young girl in a wheelchair close by
Got up, hobbled, and sat next to me.
Happy as can be, she introduced herself -
"Johanna"
She asked ME how I was doing, if I hurt my
knee?

Internally I was in disbelief,

Outwardly I told her "I had a long day!"
I asked how her day was, if she had a chance to play.
She got to meet her favorite princess, and didn't want to go to bed
We talked about where we were from (with Disney hats on our heads)
Which villa were we staying in, which ride was the best? (We couldn't agree.)
She smiled and told me "Goodnight!" I was still in disbelief.

The next morning, families gathered for breakfast.
Johanna shouted my name, not the least bit embarrassed.
All smiles again. I was so honored.
"Why was she so nice to me?" I wondered.
I told her and her family to have a great day!
That was the last thing she heard me say.

My brother has since passed, and I think of him repeatedly.
I also remember Johanna – the girl in the wheelchair – SHE approached ME!
Give Kids the World made a permanent impression on my memory.

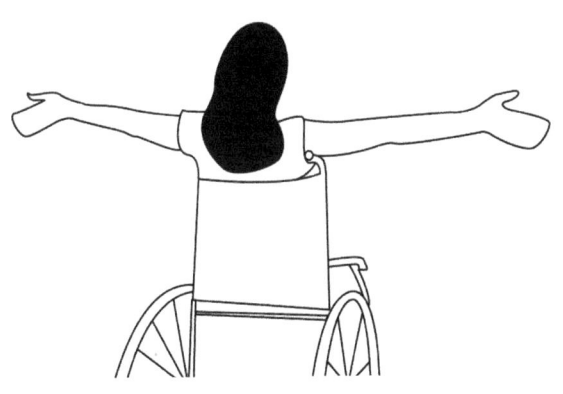

Taking A Break

WHOA

*

*

*

*

Inhale

*

*

*

Exhale

*

*

*

Inhale

*

*

*

Exhale

*

*

*

Take a look around, internally smile, and repeat

Uninvited Dinner Guest

Imagine there is a nice family dinner prepared
As you sit down, there is a knock on the door
Confused, you answer
Depression is an uninvited dinner guest

Who insists on sitting at that same table
This guest is rude, sloppy, messy, and greedy
You smile and get through dinner with this guest
Grimace inside, vow never to let them in again.

Dinner the next night
The knock is heard again
You know exactly who it is
And answer the door.

The guest is told they aren't welcome,
But they fight you, yell at you, bite you
Push and hit, ending up on the ground
Your guest makes their way to the dinner table
once again.

You're tired from the fight
Coyly join your family at the table
Watch the same rudeness, sloppiness, messiness,
and greediness
While you all sit and grin and bear it.

Every night this guest shows up at your door
Every night you battle
Same result, same result
Until one night, you reluctantly welcome them
to the table.

Son

Determined!
Fearless
Caring
Constantly turning the page
This will always be you, no matter the age

You permanently changed me I would never be
the same
Each day we pray for tools to help shape you
Into the human you need to be
For you I need strength, peace, and serious
coffee

Moms know our sons in the womb, as a human
No name, no face, no diagnosis
Your personality and preferences
We are a team, pure symbiosis

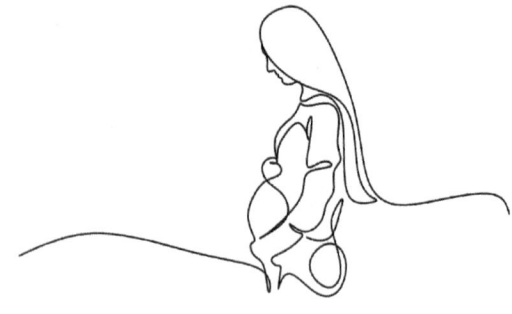

Daughter

Leader
Expressive
Tenacious
One day you'll be sage
You'll have no problem earning your wage

You permanently changed me I would never be
the same
Each day we pray for the tools to help shape you
Into the human you need to be
For you I need patience, support, and strong
coffee

I heard you calling from the other side of the
universe
Hoping I could raise a proper modern woman
In these unpredictable times
We are a team on life's expedition

Hobbies

Although people are an important asset in life
They aren't perfect, or the answer to everything
Time alone is required as well
Establish a hobby

Hobbies distract you from the old dredging of
daily life

Keep you in shape
Make you money
Keep you creative
Make you smarter
Grow your mindset

Some might do a mixture of all of the above
There is no right or wrong
Single or permanent
If it makes you happy without clocking in,
Then that is your hobby, hold it dear.

Pets

Pets are a special gift to receive
They are intuitive, you wouldn't believe.
Make sure to get the best one to match you
Make sure it's not lonely, get two!
Cute, cuddly, and funny as well
You'll glow each time you hear the collar bell.
They greet you and lick you and bother you
(You'll greet them and bother them too.)
Funny when they're curious to see what's on
your screen
In the middle of the night they might make you
scream
Loving and charming, a positive light
Can't stay mad if you want, no matter your
might
Pets are magical, wonderful, gifts
They'll keep you going when you want to call it
quits.